Poems for
Ingeborg Santor / I

Poems for Life

Ingeborg Santor
Selected and translated
by Ruth Ingram

Bibliographische Information der Deutschen National-
bibliothek: Die Deutsche Nationalbibliothek verzeichnet
diese Publikation in der Deutschen Nationalbibliographie;
detaillierte bibliographische Daten sind im Internet über
www.dnb.de abrufbar.

Herstellung und Verlag: BoD – Books on Demand,
Norderstedt

ISBN 9783753471532

Introduction

This selection of poems is the newest result of 20 years of friendship with Ruth Ingram. Nearly unbelievable it seems to me how all these years have gone by, always in contact with each other, mostly by hand-written letters first, occasional by phone, and without E-mails in those days. I feel that both of us gained a lot from our relations. But most of all I feel great gratitude for Ruth and her unusual sensitive art of translating my poetry since 2001.

A little review: In 2002, after one year of a lively correspondence, we first met in Stuttgart/Germany to discuss Ruth's first translations of my very first book of poems. Right from the beginning of our common work with two languages we knew that our understanding of poetry and our enthusiasm for poems would harmonise in a very happy way.

Several times we met in London as well as in Germany. We had bilingual readings at the Torriano Meeting House in Camden and at other literary places in London. In 2004 we got the opportunity to read at the Stuttgarter Buchwochen, a small but fine Book Fair in my home town. Of course we also visited each other during the following years. I especially like to remember our walks along the canal in Camden, Ruth always her camera at hand, taking wonderful photographs of water reflections.
The last time we met was in 2019 near Hamburg to celebrate Ruth's 90th birthday together with her German relatives and friends.

I am happy that we now again succeeded in handing over a mutual publication as exhibit of our long literary teamwork across borders and languages.

Thank you, Ruth!

Ingeborg Santor, June 2021

Through the year

7

Hier und heute

Heute, als
die Forsythien im Wind
erwachten, gelbe Schleier
in den dünnen Regen woben
zärtlichen Glanz –

heute hab ich
vergessen, dass
die Flüsse kein
Wasser mehr führen
das diesen Namen
verdiente, die Erde
nicht duftet wie
Kindheitserde, die Luft
nicht zum Atmen
geeignet ist
hier und heute

Here and today

Today as
the forsythia awoke
in the wind,
weaving tender shine
of yellow veils
in the thin rain –

today I have
forgotten that
the rivers no longer
carry water
worthy this name,
the earth has
no fragrance like
childhood earth,
the air is no longer
fit to breathe
here and today.

Aprilmorgen

Erdwärts jagt
Aprilwind das Licht
fegt mir ins Haar
seine Kühle.
Da grünt in dem frühen
Buchenlaub endlich
mein Blick, und ich laufe
ins Helle.

April morning

The April wind
pursues the light
earthwards
sweeps coolness
through my hair.
In the early
beech foliage
at last my vision
grows green and
I walk into light.

Frühlingslaune

Lerne gerade, das Wasser
zu kauen, den Wind zu trinken,
breche ab vom Brot der Bäume,
schlürfe Erdgeruch, Grasgeruch,
frühestes Licht – in der Kehle
ein blankes Gelächter.

Spring mood

Just learned to chew the water
to drink the wind,
break bread from the trees,
slurp the smell of earth, of grass,
earliest light – in my throat
a bright laughter.

Hochsommer auf Rügen

Mittag glüht Feldern
die Farben aus, mir
die Gedanken – ich fühle.
Und untauglich weiß ich
die dünne Haut
für die Stunde. Stille
lehnt schattenlos
über dem Land.

High Summer on the isle of Rügen

Midday has burnt out
all colour from the fields
and my thoughts – I feel.
And I know this thin skin
to be useless
for the hour. Stillness
leans shadowless
over the land.

Wolken-Auftritt

Da sie nicht regnen wollen, führen sie
heute ihr bestes Outfit spazieren:
opalene Roben, denen Sonnenstrahlen
von irgendwoher noch Glitzersäume
spendieren.

Nur eine, die gewichtigste, verweigert
sich dem Auftritt, schmollt in dunkelstem
Alltagsgrau – sie wird doch wohl nicht?

Ein Wind greift ein, schiebt sie sachte
den anderen zu – und auf einmal legt
die eben noch so schlecht Gelaunte
ein kleines Rouge auf, rettet die Show,
kann kein Wässerchen trüben.

Cloud Performance

As they don't want to rain they
now parade their best outfit to-day:
opal robes, still receiving sunbeams
giving them gleaming seams.

Only one cloud, the heaviest, denies
itself this performance, sulks in darkest
every-day grey – is it going to?

A wind pushes it gently towards
the others – and suddenly,
the just so bad-tempered, lays on
a little rouge and rescues the show,
nothing can dim her mood now.

Störung

Regen hat sich
müdgefallen
nistet träg
in meinen Haaren.

Weg entlang
im Tropfenglimmer
lodern Rosen
unbeirrt
und will der Abend
Stille wagen.

Nur
die Motorsäge
schreit auf
in gewesenen Wäldern.

Disturbance

Rain has tired
itself falling,
nests lazily
in my hair.

Along the way
in rain-drop gleam
roses blaze
unperturbed,
and the evening
dares stillness.

Only
the mechanical saw
screams where once
there were forests.

Gewesen

Da war
ein Garten. Fliederblaues
Blühen über Bank und Tisch.
Und Stimmen manchmal,
fremdes Wort aus
dunklem Mund, ein Lachen

Da war
ein Wachsen: rosensattes
Wuchern über Zaun und Tür,
den Augen freundlich.
Kleine Töne
federleicht ins Helle.

Da war
ein Haus auch, grau verwittert,
hinter Fensterglas
ein Schweben, weiß.

Stein wuchs drüber.
Ist gewesen.

There was

a garden. Lilac-blue
blooms over bench and table.
And sometimes voices,
foreign words from
dark mouth, a laugh.

There was
a growing, rose-deep
rampant over fence and door,
friendly to the eyes.
Little sounds
featherlight in sun.

There was
a house too, weathered grey,
behind a windows' gleam
a floating, white.

Stones covered it.
It was.

Auf den Löwenbrunnen
des Giuseppe Valadier *

Er schlug ihn aus dem Stein, diesen für immer
ruhenden Löwen. Kein König der Wildnis,
ein gefügig, ein nützlich gemachtes Tier,
weggemeißelt alles Raue, Fremde, die Ohren
Menschenohren, menschlich die geneigten
Nasenlöcher – nie haben sie Weite gewittert,
den Duft eingesogen der Savanne...

Aber kannte Valadier denn lebende Löwen?
Menschen kannte er, und kannte sie gut. Wusste,
dass sie Natur nur gebändigt ertragen, ihre
Geschöpfe bezwungen und unterwürfig.
(Wie auch er untertan war seinem päpstlichen
Auftraggeber.)

So zähmte er den Löwen seiner Imagination,
gab ihm – wen höhnte er da? – ein nacktes
Altmännergesicht. Von der Mähne ließ er ihm
den Latz ums Kinn, darüber kein Maul, ein
gespitztes Mäulchen bloß... Nie wird dieser
Löwe den Rachen aufreißen, weit, und
zu markerschütterndem Gebrüll.

* Italienischer Architekt und Städtebauer (1762-1839);
sein berühmtestes Werk ist dieser Brunnen auf der
von ihm neu gestalteten Piazza del Popolo, Rom.

Giuseppe Valadier's
Lion Fountain *

He worked him out of stone, this forever
resting lion. No king of the wilderness,
a docile, useful domestic animal, chipped away
everything rough, foreign, the ears human ears,
human the inclined nostrils – never have they
scented the wide distance, never breathed in
the smell of the Savannah...

But did Valadier know living lions?
He knew humans, and knew them well,
knew that they only tolerate tamed nature
its creatures subdued and subservient.
(Just as he was subservient to his papal
commissioner.)

So he tamed the lion of his imagination,
gave him – whom did he mock with this? –
a naked old man's face. From the mane he
left him only a bib around his chin, and
over it no mouth, only a little pointed snout...
Never will this lion tear open his jaws
to bellow an earth-shaking roar.

* Italian architect and town planner (1762-1839);
his most famous work is the Lion Fountain on the
Piazza del Popolo (Rom) which he had redesigned.

Ergo

Schlechte Zeiten
für Gedichte –
sagt man mir.

Schlechte Zeiten
also für eine
die das warme
Herz der Worte
noch nicht begrub
im Labyrinth der kühlen,
grauen Windungen
des Gehirns.

Ergo

Bad times
for poems –
I'm told.

Bad times
then for her
who has not yet
buried the warm
heart of words
in the cool, grey
convoluted labyrinth
of the brain.

Fang

Der Tag streicht die Segel –
ich aber zapple noch
in den Wanten: Festzurren
will ich, was ungesichert
flattert im Wind.

Wie er die Launen wechselt,
meiner Mühen spottet...

bis ich einstimme
ins Gelächter der Möwen
unterm gedimmten Himmel
die Hände tatenlos.
Da fällt mir rundgolden
der Abend ins Netz.

The catch

The day hauls down sails –
but I still grapple
with the shrouds: I want
to fasten tightly what
flaps unsafely in die wind.

How his moods change
he mocks my efforts...

until I join
the laughter of the gulls
under the dimming sky
my hands let go.
Then round and golden
the evening falls
into my net.

Zu früh

September hat
mit kalten Regenmessern
mir den Sommer
abgeschnitten
spricht täglich das
Novemberwort aus:
grau.
Ich lauf mi bangen
hastig-kurzen Schritten
der Wärme nach
die flieht, dem Rot
dem Blau
dem Sonnengelb
der hellen Gärten.
Doch Rost frisst
schon die Blätter an
und in den Morgennebel
hacken Krähen
schwarze Fährten.

Ich schau
als müsste ich
ertrinken:
Den letzten Schwalben
glaub ich ihre
Mittagsrufe nicht.
Ich sehe nur
die alten, grauen
Weiden winken:
Der Sommer stirbt –
als stürbe in mir
dein Gesicht.

Too early

September has
cut off the summer
with cold knife-like rain,
and daily spells
the November word:
grey.
I run with anxious
hasty steps
after the warmth
that's fled,
the red, the blue,
the sun-yellow
of bright gardens.
But early rust
eats at the leaves
and in the morning mist
crows pick out
black traces.

I gaze
as if departing,
don't believe
the last swallows'
midday calls.
I only see
the old grey
willows motion:
The summer dies –
as if in me
your face was dying.

Nachricht

Wo die Stadt
im Offenen endet,
lacht der Wind noch
über Wiesen, Feldern
sich ins Fäustchen,
atmet die Erde noch
Wärme aus. Sommer
wirft eine Handvoll
Schwalben ins Blaue.

Am Abend aber
fröstelst du, empfängst
mit hochgezogenen Schultern
verschlüsselte Nachricht.

Message

Where the town
ends in the open
the wind still laughs
over meadows
and fields
the earth still
breathes out warmth.
Summer throws
a handful of swallows
into the blue.

But in the evening
you shiver, receive
with drawn shoulders
encoded message.

November-Blues 2020

Was Zeitungen schwarz auf Weiß
berichten, das Radio über den Äther
schickt (...ach, das schöne alte Wort,
seine wolkenlose Himmelsweite...)
– es droht mir den Tag zu vergällen.

Ans Fenster flüchten: da draußen
vielleicht noch Abschied nehmende
Vogelstimmen irgendwo im Gebüsch,
ein Sonnenstrahl auf letztem Blattgold,
eine kleine Lichtmusik?

Zu spät.
Nebel zieht den Vorhand zu, sperrt
Farben und Töne aus. Und mich ein.

November Blues 2020

What the newspapers report
black on white, the radio
sends over the airwaves
"Oh, this cloudless wide sky!"
it threatens to poison my day.

Rushing to the window. Outside
perhaps still departing bird voices,
somewhere in the bushes,
a sunbeam on the last leaf-gold,
a little music of light?

Too late.
Mist draws the curtains, locks
colours and sounds out, and me in.

Dieser Herbst

Unbeirrbar, dieser Herbst! Und macht's wie immer:
Weckt die Farben auf, die unterm Blattgrün schliefen,
zieht, mit der tief gestellten Sonne verbündet, alle
Beleuchtungsregister: Wald, Gärten, Felder rückt er
in dieses Licht, das nur er kann – kein Frühling,
kein Sommer, Winter schon gar nicht. Nur er.

Und ich will es sehen, will schauen, nichts als Auge
will ich sein für das rot-orange-gelbgoldene Lodern,
den in Brand geratenen Ahorn, den hell angestrahlten
Tanz der Birken, die Glut der letzten Birnbaumblätter.
Will auch die Luft sehen, die so durchsichtig ist
wie sonst nie, will sie einatmen, als wäre sie rein.

Hören, was der Herbst sagt, will ich nicht. (Nein,
nicht wieder sein Memento...) Doch auf dem
Waldweg hat er mich schon überlistet: knistert
und raschelt unter meinen Schuhen, damit ich
ja nicht übersehe, was übrig bleibt von allem Glanz.

This autumn

Imperturbable, this autumn! He does like he always does:
wakes up the colours that slept under the leaf-green,
together with the low-set sun he uses every light register:
moves forest, gardens and fields into this illumination
that only he can do, no spring, no summer, certainly not
winter. Only autumn.

I want to see it, want to look, want to be nothing
but eyes for that red-orange-golden-yellow flame,
for the maple tree on fire, the sunbeams bright dance
on the birches, the last glow on the pear tree leaves.
I want to see the air too, that is so transparent like at
no other time, and want to breathe it in, as if it were clear.

I don't want to hear what the autumn says (no, not
again his memento mori...), though on the forest path
he has already outwitted me: it crunches and rustles
under my shoes, so that I cannot fail to see what will
remain of all this brilliance.

Herbsträtsel

Am grauen Wegrand schmales
Gesträuch: rund seine Blätter
und grün – ein blank geputztes,
ein herrisches Grün – mitten
im herbstfarbenen Wald.

Aber die Blattränder schwarz,
schwärzer als schwarz.

Welches Feuer
hat sie so gerahmt?

Autumn question

At the grey edge of the path
a small shrub with round green
leaves – a polished shiny,
lordly green – in the midst
of autumn coloured wood.

But at the leaves edges black,
blacker as black.

What fire has
framed them like this?

Wintersaat

Wörter säe ich aus
im schwindenden Licht,
dass sie keimen
unterm Schnee
und irgendwann
rüberwachsen
aufs leere Blatt.

Winter Seed

I sow out words
in fading light,
for them to sprout
under the snow
and sometime
to grow over onto
the empty page.

In and out of Love

Dieses Wort: Lapislazuli

Wenn ich mich
davonmachte: Wer
sollte des Löwenzahns
Dennoch
besingen im Schutt
dieser Stadt?
Wer
sollte ein ABER
noch schreien
angesichts dieser
geschundenen Erde?
Wer die Liebe
wortwörtlich benennen
eh sie verramscht wird
zu Schlussverkaufspreisen?
Wer denn, wenn ich
mich davonmachte,
sollte dein Lächeln
bezeugen –
und wer dieses
Wort Lapislazuli
retten vorm Untergang?

This Word: Lapislazuli

If I left: who
should serenade
the dandelions defiance
in the rubble
of this town?
Who
should shout a „BUT"
in the face of this
abused earth?
Who should spell out
and name love
before it is reduced
to end-of-sale-prices?
Who then, when I left,
should witness your smile
and who rescues this
word Lapislazuli
before it is doomed?

Blickwechsel

Was kreuzt sich da, wenn
keine Insel in Sicht ist
nur Bläue?
Ins Strudeln geraten
die tiefren Gewässer
Stromschnellenland
hebt sich und sinkt
grundlos ins Dunkle
am anderen Ufer.

Exchanging looks

What can meet there
where no island
is in sight, only blue?
In deeper waters
currents give rise
to new land
that sinks bottomless
into the dark
on the other shore.

Vorübergehend

Manchmal baust Du mir
aus Worten
absichtslos ein Nest
in deine hohle Hand.
Fast könnte ich da
– vorübergehend –
heimisch werden.

In passing

Sometimes, without
intent, you build for me
a nest out of words
in the hollow of your hand.
Almost – in passing –
I could be at home there.

Kein Zutritt

Lang schon irre ich
umher im Schilderwald
vor deinem Garten:
Parken ist hier
nicht erlaubt
und ich soll nicht
begehren
meines Nächsten
Herzgedanken
noch Hand.

Auch der Blick
übern Zaun auf die
blaue Traumwiese ist
nur hin und wieder
bei Wohlverhalten
gestattet.

Komme ich aber
dem Tor zu nahe
buchstabierst du
verschlossnen Gesichts:
Zutritt verboten.

No Admission

I have been lost
for a long time
in the forest of signs
before your garden:
parking is not allowed here
and I should not
desire my nearest one's
heart-felt thoughts
nor hand.

Also looking
over the fence onto
the blue dream-meadow
is only permitted
with good behaviour.

But if I come
too near to the gate
your closed face
spells out:
Entry forbidden.

Granit

Dein Wort fiel
zwischen uns
schlug auf
blieb liegen.

Ein harter Brocken
und zu groß, als dass
andere Worte je
ihn überstiegen.

Granite

Your word fell
between us
hit the ground
and was left lying.

A hard piece
too large
for other words
ever to overcome.

Hellsicht

Wie wetterwendisch der Wind heute weht, schickt
Regen, schickt Schnee, plötzlich gleißende Bläue,
treibt Wolkenlämmer, bis unversehn's eine Faust
sich ballt, anschwillt und über mir stehn bleibt,
als wär ich gemeint.

Und wenn sie auch blendet vor Weiße:
sie droht mir. Warum?
                                    Weil ich es sehe.

Second Sight

How changeable the wind blows today,
blows rain, blows snow, and suddenly
glittering blue, drives fleecy clouds,
till without warning a fist clenches,
swelling, it stays above me as if
meant for me.

Though it's whiteness is dazzling:
it threatens me. Why?
                                    Because I see it.

Und wieder

Nicht gezählt
wie oft vergebens:
Sehnsucht erschlagen
und Hoffnung erwürgt
mit den eigenen Händen,
ausgerissen wie Unkraut
die sanften
Blüten der Lust.
Mich dem Alltag
an den Hals geworfen
ins graue Lotterbett,
den kalt gezeugten
Bastard Trauer
ertränkt in Vergessen.

Wieder und wieder
aber wuchsen die
versengten Flügel
neu, und wieder
wieder
umkreise ich
brennend die helle
Flamme.

And again

Not counted
how often in vain:
killed my longing
and strangled hope
with my own hands,
torn out like weeds
the gentle blossoms
of pleasure.
Thrown myself
into the daily grind,
the bastard grief,
begotten in die cold
grey dissolute bed,
drowned in forgetting.

But again and again
my singed wings grew,
and again
– still burning –
I circle
the bright flame.

Ausgeträumt

Nicht gerne, aber
was sein muss endlich
zusammengekehrt
aus staubigen Winkeln
bedachtsam
ins Helle geschoben:
ins Winterlicht vor
meinen anderen Blick.

In den entleerten
Herzkammern zieht's.

Finished dreaming

Not willingly, but
it had to be done
at last. Swept out
from the dusty corners
thoughtfully
pushed into the open:
into the winter-light
to be seen
with other eyes.

In the emptied
heart-chambers
there is a draught.

Niemand da

Da ist niemand.
Längst verloren.
Oder übersehen
nicht erkannt
vorbeigegangen
weggeschickt.
Oder:
nie geboren.

Keine Antwort also.
Niemand da.
Keiner.

No-one there

There is no-one.
Long lost
or over-looked
not recognized
gone past
sent away.
Or:
never born.

So no answer.
No-one there.
None.

Winterliedchen
(Mäßig bewegt)

Hast, mein Lieb
mich längst verlassen,
friert ein schmaler
Baum im Wind.
Vor dem Fenster
flehn die blassen Wort-
gespenser, nebelblind.

Bist, mein Lieb
so weitgegangen,
aber gingst
nie weit genug.
Wankt der Baum
und fühlt die bangen
Früchte fallen, die er trug.

Hast, mein Lieb
mich lang verlassen,
bricht ein kahler
Baum im Wind.
Vor dem Fenster
wehn die nassen Wort-
gespenster. Nacht beginnt.

Little winter song
(moderato, ma non troppo)

Long you have left me, love
a small tree freezing
in the wind.
Pale ghost-words
entreat, blind in mist
before my window.

You went far, my love
but never far enough.
Tree sways in the wind,
feels the frightened
fruits it carried fall.

Long you have left me, love
a bare tree
breaks in the wind.
Before my window
blow the rain-soaked
word-ghosts. Night begins.

„Volverlo a ver"
In memoriam Gabriela Mistral *

Du, andere
hast meinen Schrei geschrien
der in mir tief
so lange schlief.

Kein Ton
kommt über meine Lippen.
Aber mein Gesicht
schreit dein Gedicht

* Chilenische Dichterin (1889-1957),
Nobelpreisträgerin 1945

„Volverlo a ver" *
(I want to see him again)

You, unknown one
have cried my cry
that deep in me
has slept so long.

No tone
passes my lips
but my face cries
your poem.

* Title of a poem by Gabriela Mistral (1889-1957),
Chilean Poet, Nobel prize winner 1945

Zuletzt

Es ist alles gesagt.
Deine stummen Hunde
hetzten längst
mein letztes Wort
zu Tode.

Pfeif sie zurück:
Vom versteinten Gefühl
ist kein Hausfriedensbruch
mehr zu fürchten.

Atme auf.
Schließ die Tür.
Lösch das Licht.

Es ist alles gesagt.

At last

Everything has been said.
Your mute dogs
have long hounded
my last word to death.

Whistle them back.
There is no need to fear
trespass from my feelings
now turned to stone.

Breathe easy.
Shut the door.
Put out the light.

Everything has been said.

Dann aber

Atmen.
Sich regen in der
fast schon zersprengten
Puppenhülle.
Abschwören dem dunklen
Vatergott dreimal,
ehe der Hahn kräht.
Dem dämmernden Morgen
das Herz entgegen werfen
aus der sterbenden
Larvenhaut.
Nur einmal noch
zügeln die Freude
der bebenden Flügel –

dann aber:
schimmernder, tanzender
Taumel ins Licht!

But then

To breathe.
To move
in the nearly fractured
chrysalis.
Forswear the dark
father-God three times,
before the cock crows.
Throw the heart
out of the dying cocoon
toward the dawning morning.
Only once more
restrain the joys
of trembling wings –

but then:
shimmering, dancing
tumble into the light!

Staying Alive

Menetekel

Ein kleiner Vogel
schlug mitten im Flug
krachend mir gegen
die Fensterscheibe.

Ab stürzte er
fassungslos aus
dem widergespiegelten
Himmel –
den Flügel gebrochen
das Herz
oder beides.

Am Fensterglas
klebt nun
ein winziger Tropfen
rötlich.
Und zarter noch
– kaum zu benennen –
ein Etwas, das vorher
Flaum war vielleicht
an pochender Kehle

Menetekel

A little bird
struck against my
window-pane
in mid flight
and crashed.

Bewildered, it fell
out of the
mirrored sky,
its wing broken,
its heart
or both.

Now, a tiny reddish drop
sticks on the window-glass.
And more delicate still
– hardly to be
distinguished –
a something which
previously perhaps
was some down
on a pulsating throat.

Drahtseilakt

Am stachelbewehrten Maschendrahtzaun
einer Wiese entlang, ganz in Gedanken.
Auf einmal im Augenwinkel Irritation:
eine Bewegung. War's eine Bewegung?

Ich stehe, sehe – und kann es nicht glauben:
Zwischen den Stacheln zwei tastende
Fühler, ein bewohntes, zart gebändertes
Schnirkelschneckenhaus!

Wie nur ist sie über all das Glatte, Kalte
so hoch hinauf gelangt? Eine Gipfelstürmerin,
geduldig dabei, sich und ihr schwankendes
Rucksack-Haus auszubalancieren. Aber –

Pass auf, du stürzt ab!
Ich kann's nicht länger mit ansehen, greife
das Häuschen, ziehe es samt Bewohnerin
vorsichtig vom Draht, setze es in Gras.

Und begreife im Weitergehen: Eben
habe ich eine Karriere verhindert – die
Erfüllung eines Traums vom Seiltanz...

Barbed Wire Act

Walking along a field with a barbed
wire fence deep in thought. Suddenly
an irritation in the corner of my eye –
a movement. Was it a movement?

I stand still, look – and can't believe it:
between the barbs two feelers out of
a small coiled shell, the inhabitant
sensing its way forward.

How did it get so high up over all that
cold wire with no foothold, making
an assault on the summit, balancing
itself with the swaying backpack.

Look out, you'll fall off!
I can't watch it any longer, take the shell
together with the occupant, pull it gently
from the wire down into the grass.

As I walk on, I realize: I have just
prevented the fulfilment of a dream
to become a high wire dancer.

Schattenflug

Einmal, ein einziges Mal nur sah ich sie
im Dämmerlicht nebeneinander sitzen
auf einer Schranke zwischen Feldweg
und altem Bauernhaus, sah ihre dunklen,
rundäugigen Gesichter reglos mir zugewandt.

Mein Stehenbleiben, mein Schauen raubt
ihnen die Ruhe – auf lautlosen Schwingen
heben sie ab, ein zwiefacher Schattenflug,
der eins wird mit Waldranddunkel.

Shadow Flight

Once, the only time I saw them
in the dusk, sitting next to each other
on a gate between field path and
an old farm house, saw their dark
round-eyed faces motionless turned
towards me.

My standing still, my looking, robbed
them of their rest – on soundless wings
they lifted off, a double shadow flight
that became one with the darkness
of the wood's edge.

Live-Konzert

Eine Amsel auf dem höchsten aller Firste
eröffnet ihr A-capella-Konzert, schmettert
neueste Arien, trillert, jubiliert, lässt ihre Kehle
beben, ist purer Gesang.

Eine Diva ohne Zweifel, auf einsamer Höhe,
eine Meisterin Schwindel erregender
Koloraturen – weithin zu hören: einzig sie.

Als ich wieder aufschaue, balanciert sie
eine Etage höher auf einer TV-Antenne –
um kein Jota weniger innig und souverän.

Der First hat wohl nur als Probebühne gedient
– jetzt ist die Primadonna auf Sendung.

Live Concert

A blackbird on the highest of all ridges
opens a Concert a capella, sings out
her newest arias, trills, jubilations, lets
her throat vibrate in pure song.

A diva, without doubt on lonely height,
a mistress of dizzying coloratura
to be heard far away – her alone.

As I look up again, she balances
one floor above on a TV aerial –
no less passionate and sovereign.

The ridge was only a rehearsal stage
– now the prima Donna is on air.

Stadtvögel

Dass Nachtigallenmännchen in Berlin
gegen den Verkehrslärm nicht ansingen
können, sondern schreien müssen – und
sie tun's mit bis zu 95 Dezibel – ist schon
länger bekannt. Ob ihre lautstarke Balz
den anzulockenden Weibchen gefällt,
wurde nicht untersucht. Doch bekommt
das alte Lied „Wenn die Nachtigallen
schlagen" nicht eine ganz neue Bedeutung?

Stuttgarts städtische Amseln haben sich
anderes einfallen lassen: Täuschend echt
flöten sie Handy-Klingeltöne – wissen sie,
dass wir uns melden und nichts verstehen?
Singen hören kann man sie auch: Noch
nachts um zehn schmettern sie laut
von Kaufhausdächern herab in kunstlicht-
grelle Straßen. Halten sie die aufsteigende
Wärme von da unten für Frühlingswehen?

Tauben in Hamburg mögen es besonders
kommunikativ: Mit Vorliebe morgens um vier
beginnen sie auf möglichst hohen Giebeln
Gespräche mit ihresgleichen. Über ihr Gurren
könnte man noch hinweg hören, vielleicht
sogar wieder einschlafen – würde nicht
der letzte Ton ihrer Kadenzen in die Höhe
geschraubt und da oben in der Schwebe
bleiben als unerlöstes Fragezeichen.

In welcher Stadt auch immer: Ganz und
gar nicht zu überhören ist das harte
Gelächter der Elstern – sie haben, was
akustische Präsenz angeht, wohl von jeher
den Schnabel vorn.

City Birds

Because nightingales can no longer
sing against the traffic noise in Berlin,
they have to shout – and they do it
up to 85 decibels – that's already known
for some time. If their loud courtship pleases
their females has not been researched;
but the old folk song: "Wenn die Nachtigallen
schlagen" now gets a quite new meaning.

Stuttgart's city blackbirds have had
a different idea: they imitate whistling tones
of mobile phones – do they know that we
will answer, and understand nothing?
We can hear them sing, too: Still at ten
at night they sound loudly from high roofs
down into artificially glaring light streets.
Do they take the rising heat down there
for spring wind?

Pigeons in Hamburg like communicating
especially in the early morning: At four o'clock
they begin conversations with their own kind,
mostly on highest gables. One could still shut out
their cooing, perhaps even go to sleep again,
if the last tone in their cadences were not
twisted into greater height, and up there
hovering stay like an unsolved question mark.

In whatever city, not to be shut out
from your ears is the magpie's hard laughter.
They have, what acoustic ability is concerned,
always first place.

Schritte

Gestern
als meine Zukunft
ein Kind war
ist mir die Zeit
zersprungen unterm
leichtfertigen Fuß.

Die Scherben
sammle ich heute
behutsamen Schrittes
komme alltäglich
dem Morgen zuvor.

Steps

Yesterday
when my future
was a child
time fractured
under my
careless foot.

To-day
I collect the fragments
treading carefully
every day, step ahead
of tomorrow.

Treibgut

Weggeflossen
unter den Händen
der Tag. Am Abendufer
angespült Reste
einer unsinkbaren
Hoffnung.

Driftwood

The day floated away
under my hands.
On the banks
of the evening
remains of
an unsinkable hope.

Zweierlei

Das ist doch fantastisch,
– sagte ich zum Arzt –
wenn Herz und Hirn so
musikalisch sind, dass sie
sogar Synkopen beherrschen!

Vom Djembé-Trommeln wisse ich,
wie schwierig es sei, unbetonte
Schläge zu betonen, um den Takt
aufzubrechen, dem Rhythmus
mehr Drive zu geben!

Aus dem Konzept gebracht,
sah er mich an – musikalisch
habe er das Wort nicht gemeint...

Schon gut, sag ich, hab nur versucht,
es etwas harmloser zu deuten.
Und wissen Sie: Ich lebe von Wörtern.
Besonders von doppeldeutigen.

Two possibilities

But that is fantastic
– I said to the doctor –
when heart and brain
are so musical, that they
master syncopation!

I knew from Djembe-drumming
how difficult it is to stress
unstressed beats, in order
to break the rhythm
and give it more drive!

Brought out of his concept
he looked at me – musical?
He hadn't meant the word…

All right, I said, I only tried to make
the meaning a little more harmless.
And you know: I live from words.
Especially from ambiguous ones.

So viel Mut

Flagge zeigen:
Weißes Haar
nicht übertünchen mehr
mit falschem Blond
nicht weglächeln wollen
den bitteren
Zug um die Lippen
und nicht mehr
ver-scherzen
den Schmerz.

Sagen:
Ja, ich bin
sehr allein.

So viel Mut
hätte ich gern.

So much courage

Show the flag:
White hair
no longer to be
touched up
with false blond,
not wishing to smile
away the bitter line
around the lips
and not joke away
the pain.

Say:
Yes, I am
very alone.

So much courage
I would like to have.

Was, wenn?

Wie schräg der Mond hängt
über schrägen Dächern – und
zeigt nicht sein Gesicht. Vielleicht,
dass er längst schon
sich abgewandt hat vom blauen
Planeten, nicht länger gewillt,
anzuschauen, was wir treiben
hier unten, und wie so Vieles
schwindet, das zu bescheinen
er gewohnt war? Vielleicht,
dass er bald überhaupt
nicht mehr Trabant sein will
dieses von Menschen bewohnen
Himmelskörpers und sich losreißt
zu einer Reise möglichst weit weg
ins All?

What, when?

The moon hangs at a slant
over slanting roofs – and
doesn't show his face. Perhaps
that he has long since
turned away from the blue
planet, no longer willing
to look on what we do
down here, and how much
is disappearing, that he used
to shine on. Perhaps
that he very soon doesn't want
to be a satellite any more
for this planet, inhabited
by humans, and tears himself free
for a journey as far away
as possible into the universe?

Neues vom Schnee, vom Glück

Entdeckt in meinen Wörterschachteln die Zeile:
„The snowy grounds of happiness". Aus welchem
Zusammenhang gerissen, angeeignet von wem?
Kein Erinnern. Aber der Klang der fremd-vertrauten
Sprache gleich im Ohr. Und hartnäckig präsent
den Tag lang, im Einschlafen noch.

Warum snowy? Landschaften des Glücks
verschneit, zugeschneit, eingeschneit? Oder
ganz anders zu deuten? „In einem kühlen Grunde" *
fällt mir ein – als wär's ein Ort unterm Schnee
und dort verborgen das Glück, gut geschützt.
Untergründig das Glück, nicht offensichtlich.

Spät nachts aufgewacht, denke ich wieder
der Zeile nach. Gehe irgendwann ans Fenster,
einer Ahnung wegen – und wirklich: Es schneit!
Schneit lautlos über the grounds of happiness hin.
Und über zwei Sprachen, die schweigen sich aus.

* Gedicht von Joseph von Eichendorff (1788 – 1857),
vertont 1840 von Wilhelm Glück

News of Snow, of Happiness

This line, found in my collection of phrases:
"The snowy grounds of happiness". In what connection
and from whom was it taken, and then owned by me?
I have no memory of it. But I had the sound of the familiar
foreign language immediately in my ear, and it was
stubbornly present all day, still when going to sleep.

Why snowy? The landscapes of happiness snowed
under, covered, simply disappeared? Or quite
differently to interpret? „In einem kühlen Grunde" *
comes to mind, as if it were a place under the snow,
and there hidden happiness, well protected.
Below ground happiness, not evident.

Awake, last night I think again about the line,
go to the window some time later because of
an apprehension – and really: it snows! Snows
soundlessly over the grounds of happiness.
And over two languages in their mutual silence.

* A poem by Joseph von Eichendorff (1788-1857), set to music
1840 by Wilhelm Glück

Darauf zu

Trockengefallen schon lang
meine Trauer; weniges wächst da
und spärlich – zu tief
sank das Wasser, die Wurzeln
darben. Vielleicht
wäre Deichbruch zu wünschen,
Gefahr: landunter?

Zu wissen: käme die Flut,
auch die Furcht stiege an
und der halb schon versandete
Mut könnte untergehn.
Aber zu wissen auch: weit
würden die Ohren wieder
sich öffnen dem Klang
des Wassers und weit
die Augen dem Tanz
des über den Wellen
zersplitternden Lichts.

Und wenn er denn bräche,
der Damm: könnt ich
den Fluten entgegen gehn, stolz
und bereit? Mehr doch als einmal
trugen sie mich, und nur
eine Handbreit war
zwischen Schweigen und Wort,
als ich sprang.

Aber gefasst sein
auf die im Strudel treibenden
Trümmern des Gestern –
Abbilder, Schemen nur, keines
ist fest und hält stand.
Ungeübt könnt ich
ins Leere greifen, geblendet
vom Leuchten der Schatten.

Mut wäre zu sagen: Komm, Flut.
Dieses durstige Land
ist kein Boden mehr
unter den Füßen – hier
warte ich unruhig und bang
"aber wie Orpheus weiß ich
auf der Seite des Todes das Leben" *

Und weiß: auch das kleinste
Gepäck wäre zu viel. Wie aber
leicht sein in diesen
ausgetretenen Schuhen
voller Sand? Abwerfen
auch sie und die alte
bequeme Haut. Eine andre
wird wachsen, tauglich
für landlose Fahrt.

* Zeilen aus einem Gedicht von Ingeborg Bachmann

Towards

My grief, already long ago
dried out; little grows there
and sparsely – the water sank
too deep, the roots suffer.
Perhaps one would wish
for a dyke-break,
the danger – flooded land?

Knowing, if the flood came
fear would rise too,
and the already half silted up
courage could drown.
But to know too, my ears
would open again wide
to the sound of water,
and the eyes to the dance
of splintered light
over the waves.

And if the dam
then broke: could I go
towards the flood, proud
and ready? More than once
it carried me, and only
a hand's breadth was
between silence and word
as I leapt.

But to be prepared
for the current's drifting
debris of yesterday's images,
only sketches, none
firm and enduring.
Unpractised, I could
grasp emptiness, dazzled
by the light of shadows.

It would be courageous
to say: Come flood. This
thirsty land is no longer
ground under my feet – here
I wait restless and anxious
"but like Orpheus I know
at the side of death is life." *

And I know: even the smallest
baggage would be too much.
But how to be light in these
worn-out shoes full of sand?
Throw them off too, and
the old comfortable skin.
A new one will grow,
usable for landless voyage.

* Lines from a poem by Ingeborg Bachmann

Ruth Ingram (born 1927 in Berlin) was formerly a psychiatric social worker and a principal lecturer and Course Director of a course in Applied Social Studies. On retiring she completed courses in screen printing, textiles, embroidery, batik as well as photography.
She exhibited textiles, original clothing and photography in various small galleries and in her own home in support of Greenpeace, Oxfam and Medicines Sans Frontieres.

She attended part-time courses at the London School of Poetry for three years and also organized poetry translation workshops (translating from French and German) in her own home for 15 years. The participants 'Camden Mews Translators' have published two anthologies: 'Over the Water' and 'Across Frontiers' both available at the poetry library at the South Bank London.

She has had two collections of translations published: 'Selected poems by Hans Sahl' and 'Selected poems by Arno Holz, as well as the Anthology 'In Exile' – poems by Hilde Domin, Mascha Kaleko and Hans Sahl. Several of her own poems and some translations appeared in six publications of the High-gate Poets in their journal 'Kites'. A long poem by Hilde Domin was published in 'Modern Poetry in Translation', and two of her translations of poems by Hans Sahl were published in 'The Fenland Reed' journal. She also translated many of the published and unpublished poems by Ingeborg Santor.

Ingeborg Santor (born in 1941 in Koblenz) was employed as editor in various publishing houses from 1966 - 1976; later she worked free-lance as editor and text-writer for museums.

She began to write in her early youth. In the sixties some of her poems and short stories first appeared in journals and newspapers. Later several poems were broadcast by Nordwestdeutscher Rundfunk, few essays and documentary features by Südwestrundfunk. In 1998 and 2003 two collections of poetry, in 1998 a collection of short stories have been published. Single of her poems as well as prose texts have been translated into Polish and appeared in literary journals and anthologies in Poland since 2004.

She herself has translated children's stories and non-fiction books from English, later she began to translate English poetry. Her poems were published in Ruth Ingram's translation in the collection 'Between languages' by Hearing Eye in 2007, together with her translations of poems by John Rety. More recently she has translated a cycle of poems by Judy Gahagan: 'Tours around the Soul of Ludwig' appeared in 2009. In 2014 another collection of her own poems entitled 'Lichtfänger' was published, in 2016 followed a story-telling book about her early childhood. A new collection of poems, 'Vom Leuchten der Schatten', was printed in 2019.

Contents / Inhalt

Index of English Titles

Twelve poems were taken from Ingeborg Santor's first col-
lection "Amsellied und Krähenschrei" (1993), thirteen from
"Im Schneelicht" (2003). Both editions are out of print. Few
of the now selected poems appeared in her books "Licht-
fänger" (2014) and "Vom Leuchten der Schatten" (2019).
The other poems are published here for the first time.

Index of German Titles